W9-CXU-270

The Nervous System

by Helen Frost

Consulting Editor: Gail Saunders-Smith, Ph.D.

Consultant: Lawrence M. Ross, M.D., Ph.D.
Member, American Association of Clinical Anatomists

Pebble Books

an imprint of Capstone Press
Mankato, Minnesota

JUN 2014

HU

Pebble Books are published by Capstone Press
1710 Roe Crest Drive, North Mankato, Minnesota 56003
www.capstonepub.com

Library of Congress Cataloging-in-Publication Data
Frost, Helen, 1949–
      The nervous system / by Helen Frost.
      p. cm.—(Human body systems)
      Summary: Simple Text, photographs, and diagrams introduce the nervous
system and its purpose, parts, and functions.
      ISBN-13: 978-0-7368-0651-0 (hardcover)
      ISBN-10: 0-7368-0651-2 (hardcover)
      ISBN-13: 978-0-7368-8779-3 (paperback)
      ISBN-10: 0-7368-8779-2 (paperback)
      1. Nervous System—Juvenile literature. [1. Nervous system.] I. Title.
II. Human body systems (Mankato, Minn.)
      QM451 .F76 2001
      611′.8—dc21   00-024558

Note to Parents and Teachers

The Human Body Systems series supports national science
standards for units on understanding the basic functions of the
human body. This book describes the nervous system and illustrates
its purpose, parts, and functions. The photographs and diagrams
support early readers in understanding the text. This book also
introduces early readers to subject-specific vocabulary words, which
are defined in the Words to Know section. Early readers may need
assistance to read some words and to use the Table of Contents,
Words to Know, Read More, Internet Sites, and Index/Word List
sections of the book.

Printed in the United States of America in Eau Claire, Wisconsin.

052013   007417R

Table of Contents

The nervous system controls the body. It helps people move and speak. It helps people think, learn, and remember.

brain

spinal cord

nerves

The brain, the spinal cord, and nerves make up the nervous system. The nervous system carries messages called signals. Signals tell the body what to do.

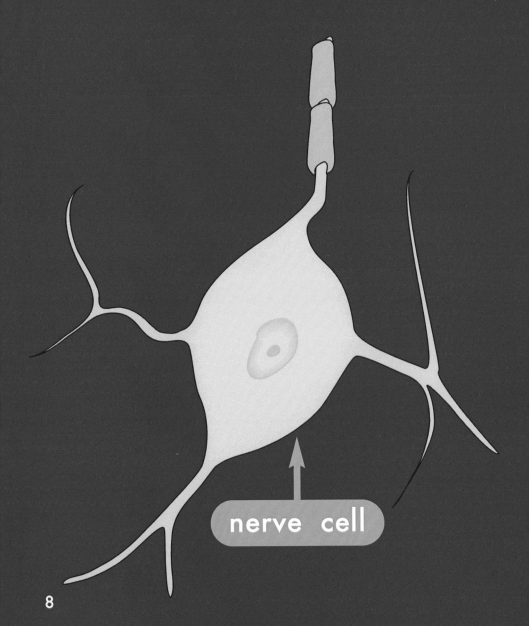

nerve cell

8

Signals travel quickly from one nerve cell to another. The brain, the spinal cord, and nerves are all made of nerve cells.

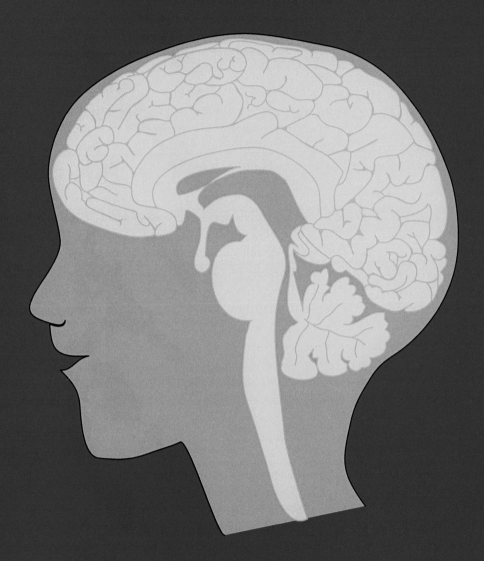

Many signals start in the brain. The signals travel from the brain to other parts of the body.

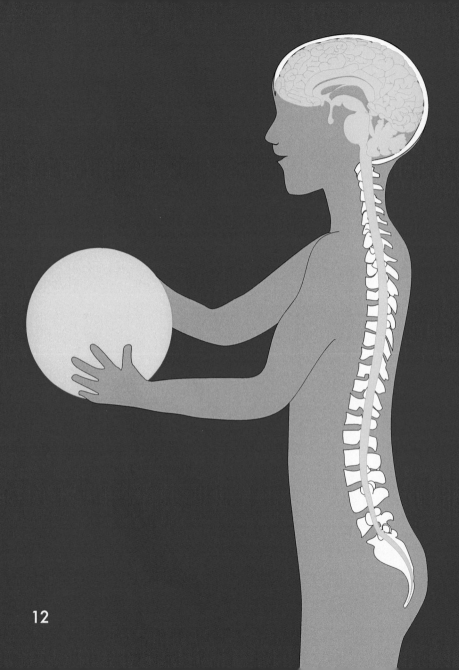

The brain is connected to the spinal cord. The spinal cord is a group of nerves in the back. Many signals travel from the brain to the spinal cord.

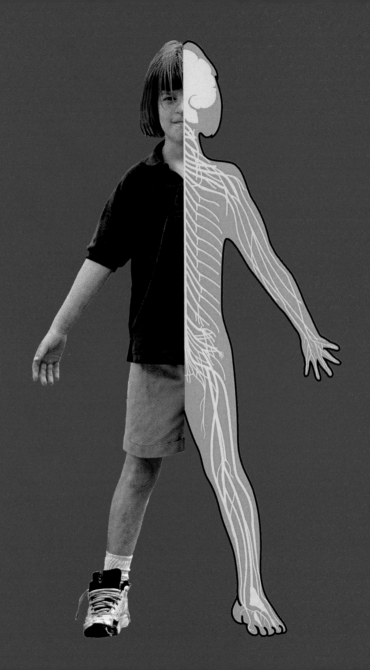

Nerves branch out from the brain and the spinal cord. These nerves then branch out into smaller nerves all over the body.

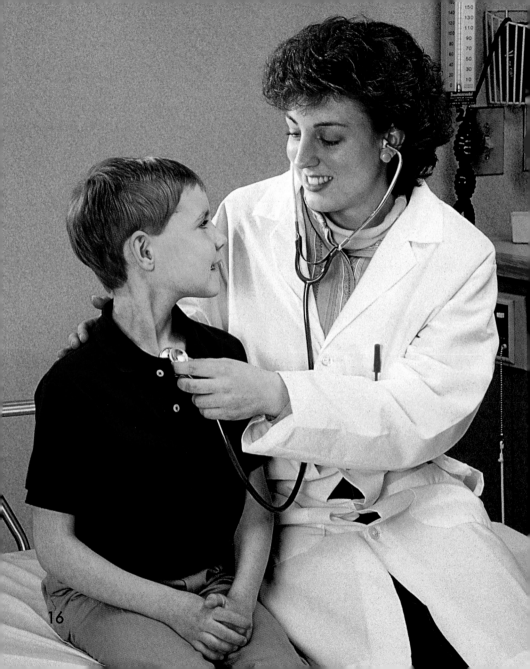

The brain controls many parts of the body. The brain sends signals to help the lungs breathe. The brain sends signals to help the heart pump blood.

Signals from the body travel to the brain. Skin may touch something cold. Nerves in the skin send this signal through the spinal cord to the brain. The brain understands that the water is cold.

The nervous system sends signals all the time. It helps all body parts work together.

Words to Know

brain—the body part in the head that controls the body; the brain helps people move, think, and feel; it controls breathing and the heartbeat.

nerve—a thin bundle of fibers that sends signals; the signals go from one part of the body to another.

nervous system—the brain, spinal cord, and nerves; messages travel through the nervous system among all parts of the body.

signal—a message; nerves carry signals to and from the brain and spinal cord.

spinal cord—a long, thick cord of nerve tissue; the spinal cord starts at the brain and goes down the back; the spinal cord carries signals between the brain and other parts of the body; the spine protects the spinal cord.

Read More

Frost, Helen. *Your Senses.* The Senses. Mankato, Minn.: Pebble Books, 2000.

Sandeman, Anna. *Brain.* Body Books. Brookfield, Conn.: Copper Beech Books, 1996.

Simon, Seymour. *The Brain: Our Nervous System.* New York: Morrow Junior Books, 1997.

Stille, Darlene R. *The Nervous System.* A True Book. New York: Children's Press, 1997.

Internet Sites

Do you want to find out more about The Nervous System? Let FactHound, our fact-finding hound dog, do the research for you.

Here's how:

1) Visit *http://www.facthound.com*

2) Type in the **Book ID** number: **0736806512**

3) Click on **FETCH IT.**

FactHound will fetch Internet sites picked by our editors just for you!

Index/Word List

Word Count: 213
Early-Intervention Level: 22

Editorial Credits
Martha E. H. Rustad, editor; Kia Bielke, designer; Marilyn Moseley LaMantia, Graphicstock, illustrator; Katy Kudela, photo researcher

Photo Credits
David F. Clobes, cover
Index Stock Imagery, 16
Jarvis Photo/Pictor, 20
Kent Knudson/Pictor, 4
Marilyn Moseley LaMantia, 14, 18
Mellott/Pictor, 1

The author thanks the children's section staff at the Allen County Public Library in Fort Wayne, Indiana, for research assistance. The author also thanks Eric Chudler, Ph.D., Research Associate Professor, Department of Anesthesiology, University of Washington, Seattle.